Dare to Dream:
The Forgotten Heroines

10 Trailblazing Female Scientists, Mathematicians, and Inventors

Siya Bhagat

Chennai • Bangalore

CLEVER FOX PUBLISHING
Chennai, India

Published by CLEVER FOX PUBLISHING 2025
Copyright © Siya Bhagat 2025
Illustrations by Falgunni Shah

All Rights Reserved.
ISBN: 978-93-67078-81-5

This book has been published with all reasonable efforts taken to make the material error-free after the consent of the author. No part of this book shall be used, reproduced in any manner whatsoever without written permission from the author, except in the case of brief quotations embodied in critical articles and reviews.

The Author of this book is solely responsible and liable for its content including but not limited to the views, representations, descriptions, statements, information, opinions and references ["Content"]. The Content of this book shall not constitute or be construed or deemed to reflect the opinion or expression of the Publisher or Editor. Neither the Publisher nor Editor endorse or approve the Content of this book or guarantee the reliability, accuracy or completeness of the Content published herein and do not make any representations or warranties of any kind, express or implied, including but not limited to the implied warranties of merchantability, fitness for a particular purpose. The Publisher and Editor shall not be liable whatsoever for any errors, omissions, whether such errors or omissions result from negligence, accident, or any other cause or claims for loss or damages of any kind, including without limitation, indirect or consequential loss or damage arising out of use, inability to use, or about the reliability, accuracy or sufficiency of the information contained in this book.

Contents

Ada Lovelace 1

Rosalind Franklin 5

Katherine Johnson... 9

Hedy Lamarr 13

Hypatia of Alexandria.. 17

Cecilia Payne-Gaposchkin 21

Marie Curie.. 25

Emmy Noether 29

Kalpana Chawla 33

Mary Anning.. 37

ADA LOVELACE

Computing Queen

*I*n an era when women's roles were restricted to planning tea parties or hosting soirees, Ada Lovelace's imagination was never at rest, always desperate for more. No amount of social expectations or gender-related biases could stop her from venturing further and further into the realm of mathematics and computing - which eventually led to her entirely transforming the world of modern code computers !

Born in 1815 to a famous poet, Lord Byron; and Annabella Milbanke, a zealous mathematician; Ada's childhood was far from ordinary for a girl of her time. Rather than spending her time slaving over finishing school or fiddling with embroidery, Ada was schooled thoroughly. In order to keep Ada away from her father's wild poetic tendencies, Ada's mother rushed to enrol her in rigorous classes for mathematics, physics, and music. Ada spent large chunks of her time pondering over various theories or designing intricate flying machines and boats.

Her mind was constantly abuzz with curiosity; she had an unrivalled thirst for knowledge.

When she was only 17, she met Charles Babbage, a professor at Cambridge University who introduced her to out of the world ideas and creations, specifically a machine named the "Analytical engine" Ada being Ada, saw immense potential in this machine; she predicted that it could be used for things far beyond simply calculations!

A bit later, an engineer wrote a paper on this calculating machine in French. Since Ada knew French, she was put to the tedious task of translating it. In the process of translating and interpreting the paper, Ada ended up writing notes three times as long as the original paper! She had carefully gone over the original notes, understanding them and adding in various of her own inputs, ideas, and theories, eventually creating the first ever computer programme.

Despite Ada's groundbreaking revelations, she didn't receive much attention for her work until long after she passed away. However, without her contributions to the field of computing, we might not even have had computers as we do today!

Unfortunately, Ada faced a number of health issues and passed away at the mere age of 36. Whilst her life may have been brief, the impact she has had on computer programming and modern-day computing is eternal.

Now, there is a programming language, Ada, named in the honour of this revolutionary woman, and every year, on the second Tuesday of October, Ada Lovelace day is celebrated in memory of Ada and to raise awareness of the roles of women in STEM!

ROSALIND FRANKLIN
DNA's Unsung Hero

Rosalind Franklin was born in London in 1920, with a mind as sharp as her determination. She spent her childhood darting around, playing hockey and cricket or pouring over arithmetic sums that most kids would shy away from. Despite having a delicate health, Rosalind excelled at school and yearned to be a scientist someday. She received a scholarship at Cambridge University, where she studied chemistry and even designed an improved gas mask for the British during World War II. However, this wasn't the pinnacle of her career in scientific discoveries; her greatest one was yet to come!

A few years later, Rosalind decided to study the structure of DNA using x-ray methods in a lab. However, her male colleagues, feeling threatened and thrown off by having a woman in their very male dominated workspace, would often isolate and undermine her. Furthermore, Rosalind was diagnosed with cancer, and her body was extremely weakened, which lead to her to nearly crawl up to her lab each day to continue work. Nevertheless, her grit never eroded away. Determined and resolute, Rosalind obtained a vital image of DNA's structure, Photo 51, which revealed its double helical structure. This photo took over 100 hours to obtain and unearthed an opening for numerous crucial scientific discoveries. After obtaining the image, Rosalind spent a year analysing the photo and framing a research paper.

However, one of her colleagues sneakily stole the photo without Rosalind noticing, and showed it to two other scientists, Watson and Crick, who were also working on analysing the structure of DNA. They exploited Rosalind's work, using Rosalind's photo to aid their own scientific discoveries. In fact, when Rosalind's paper and the Watson and Crick's papers were published in a science journal, Rosalind's paper was published after the Watson and Crick's paper, which made it seem as though Rosalind had taken inspiration from their paper even though in reality, it was the exact opposite.

Rosalind died of cancer a few years after these discoveries, and Watson, Crick, and one more scientist were awarded the Nobel Prize for "their" work, as unfortunately, Rosalind received little to no credit for her painstaking work for many years even after she passed away. Luckily, after thorough investigations were conducted and more and more people began to speak up on this brilliant scientist, quite a few people today are aware of Rosalind's work, and fight passionately for her recognition!

KATHERINE JOHNSON

Reach for the Moon

Katherine Johnson was born in 1918 to an African American family. She was born at a particularly chaotic time in history, as she faced discrimination based not just on her gender but also on her race. Despite all these challenges, Katherine always aimed for the stars. She was an exceptionally intelligent young girl and graduated from high school when she was just fourteen! She earned a degree in mathematics at the age of eighteen. She had a remarkable aptitude for mathematics and was supported fiercely by her close-knit family and her professor at university, who even created new advanced mathematics courses just for her!

After graduating university, Katherine first started off as a teacher but wanted to do something more challenging. Her burning passion led her to join a team of female African American mathematicians at NASA. She rapidly advanced through the ranks, and she played a pivotal role in America's first human carrying spacecraft, for which she calculated the trajectory, helping the mission advance, defying all gender norms and racial stigmas.

Known as the "human computer", Katherine also played a vital role with her calculations in the Apollo 11 mission, in which humanity reached the moon for the first time. In the Apollo 13 mission, her work helped the astronauts return to earth safely after an unanticipated emergency on their flight. She was immensely respected by her colleagues and the astronauts; in fact, John Glenn, a famous astronaut, specifically insisted that she verify the calculations made by the electronic computer for his orbital mission to ensure its accuracy.

Katherine's persistence and determination lead her to work at NASA for 33 years as one of their most valued mathematicians. NASA named a building in her honour, and she even received the presidential medal of freedom, the highest civilian honour in the USA. A few years ago, a movie on Katherine and a few of her fellow African American female coworkers was released, called Hidden Figures. It was after this movie that people began to recognise Katherine and her importance to America's history in space.

Katherine passed away relatively recently, at the age of 101 in 2020, but her legacy is sure to fire up young women of colour in STEM for a long time to come.

HEDY LAMARR

Hollywood Star and Inventor

Hedy Lamarr was born in 1914 to a well-off Jewish family in Austria. From a young age she displayed immense interest and strength in both the arts and the sciences. Her budding passion was spurred on by her father, with whom she often had long conversations on topics ranging from technology to the intricacies of machinery.

As Hedy grew older, however, her acting career took off and she never received a formal education in science. She soon married a wealthy Austrian manufacturer who proved to be extremely controlling, unhappy with Hedy's success. However, whilst married to him, Hedy was introduced to the world of military technology, which helped pique a keen interest in applied sciences.

To escape her unfortunate marriage, Hedy fled to Paris and then London, where she furthered her acting career, acting in various extremely revered films. However,

Hedy's scientific mind was constantly abuzz, and she set up a small invention workshop in her house where she was constantly tinkering with her latest ideas

When World War II broke out, Hedy wanted to help the United States create secure, radio-controlled devices that could greatly help communication. Thus, she collaborated with another inventor, George Antheil to help develop this system. Together, they devised a system that allowed for "frequency hopping", which meant that it would be incredibly difficult for an enemy to listen in, as the frequencies were constantly hopping from one to another. Hedy and George received a patent for their invention, and although Hedy didn't know it at the time, her invention would be the foundation of what runs our world today: Wi-Fi, Bluetooth and GPS all rely on Hedy's methodology to function

Hedy Lamarr was more than simply a pretty face: she was a revolutionary thinker and a groundbreaking inventor, creating work that is integral for our world even decades after her passing.

HYPATIA OF ALEXANDRIA

*H*ypatia of Alexandria was a mathematician, philosopher and an astronomer who lived in Egypt around 1600 years ago. She was born in Alexandria, which was a bustling hub for new knowledge, libraries and scholars at the time. Growing up surrounded by these books, ideas and fascinating people, it was impossible for Hypatia to not be interested in their ideas. Hypatia's father was also an excellent mathematician, who nurtured Hypatia's budding interest in the topic, always encouraging her to explore further and learn more.

Hypatia excelled, becoming one of the greatest mathematicians in Alexandria, even surpassing her father. She became the head of the Platonic School, which was a university in Alexandria at that time. She wrote various books, developed a more efficient way of attempting long division sums, tinkered with scientific instruments and taught a plethora of students from nations far and wide. She created tools that helped astronomers better engage with space, and in her books, she was able to explain extremely complex ideas in easy-to-understand terms. Hypatia believed that mathematics had a spiritual aspect, calling numbers the sacred language of the universe. Hypatia and her students studied the world of cosmos- the study of the universe- and explored various ideas. She always encouraged her students to think and question, which was taboo at the time.

Hypatia did not worship any particular deity, which made her university a haven that fostered inclusivity, allowing students of various religions to co-exist and collaborate amidst the political and religious turmoils at the time. Hypatia's ideas and theories were centuries ahead of her time. Although none of her teachings exist to this day, accounts written by her students or people who knew her help us understand Hypatia's life and various contributions much better.

Although Hypatia was an extremely valued scholar, educating thousands of students across continents, her ideals were extremely controversial, and while roaming the city one day, an angry mob of religious extremists brutally murdered her, under the claim that she was a witch. Despite Hypatia living centuries ago, her ideas and discoveries are crucial to understand aspects of math, science and philosophy even today, and she left an irremovable mark in the field of education, inspiring physicists and mathematicians for years to come.

CECILIA PAYNE-GAPOSCHKIN

Cecilia Payne-Gaposchkin was born in England in 1900, and loved studying science ever since she was introduced to it in school.

She went on to study physics and chemistry at the University of Cambridge, despite the societal barriers that prevented women from studying science at a higher level. She wasn't awarded a degree for her education though, as Cambridge didn't give degrees to women until 1948. Cecilia went on to obtain a graduate degree at Harvard University, being the first person to obtain a PhD in Astronomy at Radcliffe College (now a part of Harvard). Over there, she made a huge discovery while studying the stars- she found that they were made of hydrogen and helium, like the sun instead of iron and nickel, like the earth, which was the long-held belief. This may seem like a rather insignificant discovery to us, but in the field of astronomy, this information was trailblazing! It revolutionised the way astronomers study and regard space, the evolution of the stars and the sun, and helped them better understand the composition of the universe.

In fact, Cecilia's thesis on her findings is considered the greatest PhD thesis ever written in astronomy.

Despite her pioneering discovery, Cecilia was discouraged by an astronomer at Harvard, who brushed off her findings as incorrect and advised her to not publish and present them.

Four years later, however, he published a paper of his own, in which he reached the same conclusions as Cecilia. Despite him mentioning Cecilia's name in his work, she was largely disregarded and forgotten. Thus, for the most part of history, he was given credit for this discovery despite Cecilia's work that predated his.

Nevertheless, Cecilia continued to adore astronomy until she passed away. During her time as a researcher, she made over 2 million observations in space, which paved the path for stellar evolution. She became the first female full-time professor at Harvard, and the first woman to receive their own department at Harvard. Her story is one of frustration, but so much growth and discovery. Her work and dedication will always be appreciated.

MARIE CURIE

Explosively Excellent

*M*arie Curie was born to two teachers in Warsaw, Russian occupied Poland in 1867. She was a remarkably brilliant student but was prevented from pursuing higher education due to her gender. In an act of rebellion, Marie enrolled in the Floating University, which was a secret institution that helped educate Polish youth. After working as a governess, teacher, and saving enough money, Marie travelled to France where she studied at the Sorbonne in Paris, earning degrees in both physics and math. She could mostly only afford to eat bread and drink tea, and sometimes she would faint due to being near starvation.

While she was in Paris, she met Pierre Curie. With their shared love of science and discovery, they soon fell in love and got married.

Marie was inspired by Henri Becquerel's work on uranium, and while doing her own research, Marie discovered that thorium too had similar properties to uranium; they both reacted with photographic films and were unaffected by physical or chemical changes.

Marie's discovery was monumental, and while researching with Pierre, Marie found out that there was a wide assortment of elements that behaved similarly.

Pierre and Henri were nominated for a Nobel prize in physics, but no mention was given to Marie's essential contributions at all. Pierre stood up for Marie demanding recognition for her, and the three were able to share the Nobel prize that year, making Marie the first ever woman to be a Nobel laureate. Unfortunately, Pierre soon passed away due to being crushed by a horse drawn carriage. Marie engulfed herself in her research and work to cope with her grief and began to teach at the Sorbonne University in Paris as its first female professor.

In 1911, Marie won another Nobel prize, for chemistry due to her discovery of the radioactive elements polonium and radium, and her analysis of radium. This made her the first-and only- person to win a Nobel Prize in two different sciences.

She went on to open various research institutes in Poland, investigated radiation's effects on tumours, improving the medical field. However, Marie's tireless work with radiations is believed to have led to her ultimate death due to bone marrow cancer. Marie has inspired generations of female scientists and has played a pivotal role in our understanding of radioactivity in chemistry and physics till this date, cementing her role as an utterly invaluable scientist and person

EMMY NOETHER

*E*mmy Noether was born in 1882 Germany to a Jewish family. Her father was a mathematician, which influenced Emmy to take a strong interest in the same field. While she initially planned to teach English and French, she soon switched to mathematics. Despite being initially unable to enrol at university as she was a woman, Emmy persisted and was finally able to receive permission to formally enrol, studying algebraic invariants.

A few years later, Emmy was invited to join the mathematics department at the University of Göttingen, which was a major centre for math research. At the university, Emmy formulated and derived Noether's Theorem, which was an essential theorem for theoretical physics, helping in classical mechanics and quantum physics. In fact, Noether's Theorem was called one of the most important mathematical theorems every proved!

Emmy also worked marvels in the field of Mathematics, where her work in abstract algebra, and the concepts and structures she formulated, helped shape modern algebra.

Despite Emmy's incredibly useful work and findings, she was made to work without pay for several years after developing her theorem. Additionally, she had to give lectures under the name of her male colleague as the university did not allow female scholars to give lectures, regardless of their accomplishments. She was eventually even expelled from the university and had to flee to America due to World War 1 and the stigma against Jews.

Emmy's story is one of perseverance; her love for mathematics and physics ran so deep that no amount of gender bias or racial stigma could stop her from unrelentingly working on her theorems and the ideas that interested her. Now, she receives more recognition as various mathematical concepts, theorems and awards are associated with her name, and she has been named one of the greatest mathematicians of the 20th century.

KALPANA CHAWLA

Star Power

Kalpana Chawla was born in Karnal, Haryana. From an extremely young age, Kalpana found herself fascinated with the stars, the sky, and planes. Her parents readily supported Kalpana and her education, seeing great potential in this young girl. Kalpana never saw her gender or ethnicity as a burden, she continueDs to pursue her goals and dreams regardless of the social prejudices at that time.

After studying aeronautical engineering in Punjab, Kalpana wanted to learn even more about space, so she moved to the United States to pursue her academic desires. She earned a master's degree in aerospace engineering from the University of Texas, and later even did a PHD in Colorado.

Satisfied with her education, Kalpana joined NASA, and a few years later, she was selected to be an astronaut candidate. She travelled to space in 1997, as the first woman of Indian origin to reach space. While on that mission she performed vital experiments on microgravity, which contributed to a better understanding of how microgravity affects physical processes. Her research helped lead to a better understanding of these topics in the scientific and medical field. She also worked on a number ofseveral projects at NASA research centres that helped to improve aircraft performance and design.

Kalpana Chawla, born in Karnal, Haryana, grew up with a unquenchable curiosity about the stars, the sky, and airplanes. From the time she was a little girl, she dreamed of reaching the stars, a dream nurtured by her supportive parents, who recognised her immense potential.

Resolute despite the social barriers she faced due to her race and gender, Kalpana unrelentingly pursued her passion for science and engineering with determination. After earning a degree in aeronautical engineering from Punjab, Kalpana moved to the United States to further her studies. There, she earned a master's degree in aerospace engineering from the University of Texas and even completed a Ph.D. in Colorado!

Her impressive academic achievements led her to join NASA, where she began working on groundbreaking projects to improve aircraft design and performance. In 1997, Kalpana made history as the first woman of Indian origin to travel to space. While on this mission, Kalpana conducted vital experiments on microgravity, which led to various advancements in technological and medical fields!

Kalpana later undertook a second mission to space, however, this mission proved to be a great tragedy as her space shuttle disintegrated upon re-entering earth's atmosphere, killing everyone aboard the shuttle, including Kalpana.

Nevertheless, while Kalpana may have lived a rather brief life, her contributions and achievements live on as a shining, inspiring star to thousands of young girls and women who wish to pursue careers in STEM, as a reminder that they too can do whatever they set their minds to!

MARY ANNING

Fossil Hunter

*M*ary Anning was born in a small coastal town of England in 1799, to a poor family with ten children. Mary and her brother were the only children who survived till adulthood. Despite her rough conditions, Mary had a happy childhood, as her father and her would go on long walks by the cliffs, where they collected fossils and sold them to tourists. This led Mary to develop an intense passion for palaeontology, and she adored collecting fossils and making new discoveries.

Mary discovered a fossil of a marine reptile from the age of the dinosaurs when she was just twelve: the ichthyosaurus. A decade later, she uncovered the complete skeleton of another marine reptile, the Plesiosaurus. One of Mary's most groundbreaking findings was when she discovered a

Pterodactyls' fossil outside Germany, which helped to prove that flying reptiles did exist. Her work, which may have been just a fun hobby for Mary proved to be some of the most valuable contributions to the field of palaeontology at the time, and helped scientists understand ancient life on earth much better than previously.

Despite Mary's extremely valuable discoveries, Mary received nearly no recognition for her contributions, with credits always going to the male scientists who purchased her fossils. Her low economic status, lack of formal education and gender led Mary to live a tough life. Nonetheless, Mary's love for palaeontology and fossil hunting never wavered, and as of today, she is regarded as and acknowledged to be one of the greatest fossil hunters of the 19th century; her determination and curiosity made her a pioneer in palaeontology and an extremely skilled fossil hunter.

www.ingramcontent.com/pod-product-compliance
Lightning Source LLC
LaVergne TN
LVHW070939070526
838199LV00035B/656